BABA FARID JI

ISHWAR SINGH

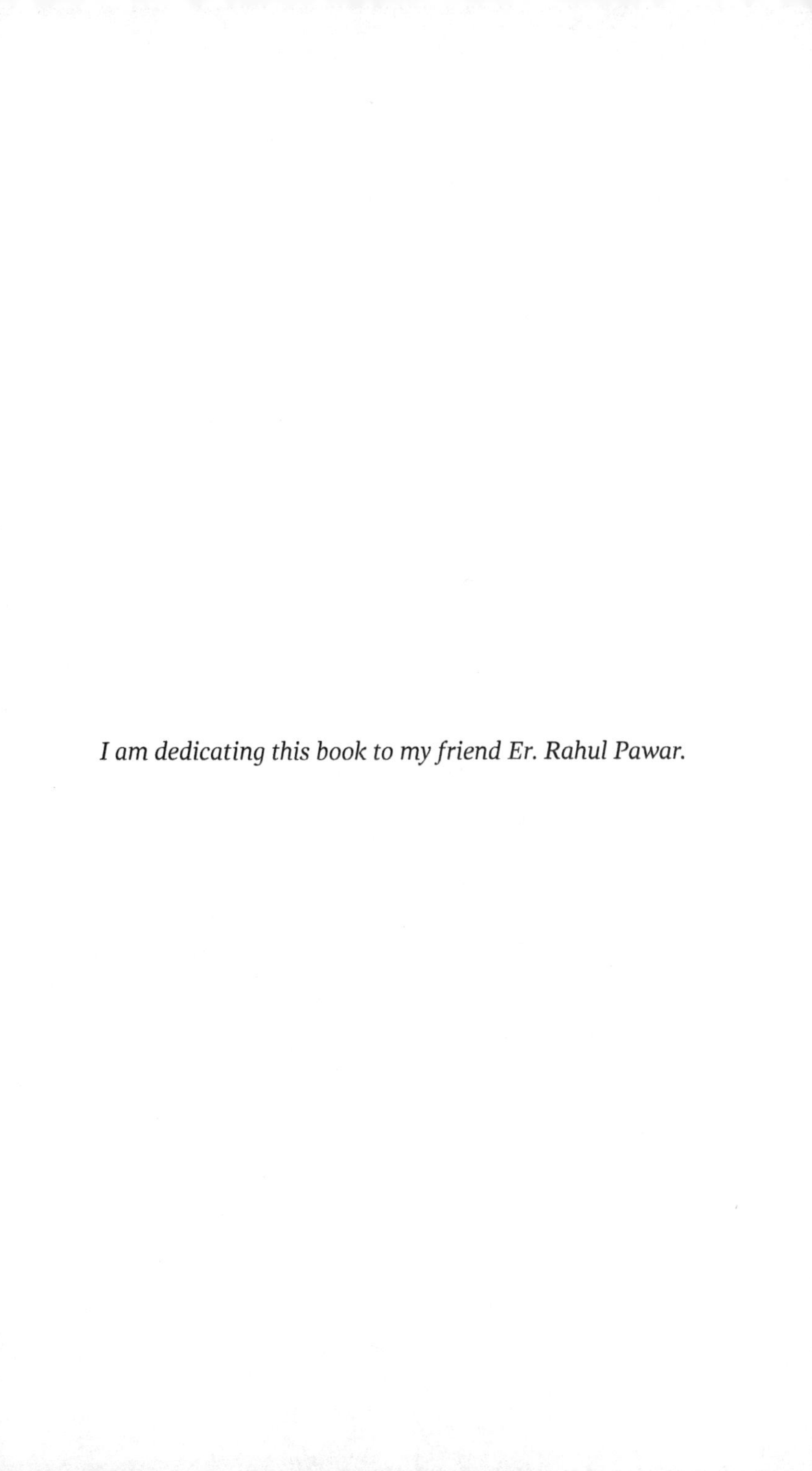

I am dedicating this book to my friend Er. Rahul Pawar.

Contents

Foreword   vii

Preface   ix

Acknowledgements   xi

Prologue   xiii

  1. Baba Farid Ji   1

Foreword

Ishwar Singh have more than ten years of experience in writing story books, sakhis of devotional saints and in research activities. He is a tremendous writer. He is doing excellent job by writing about Baba Farid Ji. He had shown very keen interest in the field of religious resources and other cultural issues.

He is also a very excellent teacher and also having deep knowledge about the social science issues. I have always seen him working very hard for his various books. He just want to express about the Indian culture to our new generations in a simple and brief manner. I wish him all the very best for his new book.

Birinder Pal Kaur

Preface

I have expressed the stories related to the life of Baba Farid Ji which I had heard from various religious personalities in my childhood. I have just tried to make this book so simple that whoever reads this book in future can understand this book easily. You will feel the story and be inspired to live the good life.

    Ishwar Singh

Acknowledgements

Writing a book is harder than I thought and more rewarding than I could have ever imagined. None of this would have been possible without my best friend, my teacher, my best motivator, my beloved mother Amarjit Kaur. She was the first who inspired me for my goals and taught me various subjects and created my interest specially in Social Sciences. She stood by me during every struggle and all my successes. Whatever I had achieved in my life it is due to my mother.

I'm eternally grateful to my father Pal Singh, who took in an extra mouth to feed when he didn't have to. He taught me discipline, tough love, manners, respect, and so much more that has helped me succeed in life. I truly have no idea where I'd be if he hadn't given me a roof over my head whom I desperately needed at that age.

To my father-in-law Narinder Singh for their moral support during the up and downs in my life. He taught me how to live positive even in the worst situations by sharing his personal experiances. He is the man who suggest me to write a book in your life because it will be your book by which you will be remembered in future.

Prologue

India is a country of vast cultural diversities. This diversity has its roots in the ancient and medieval periods of history. In the present life every person is playing his role according to the role given by nature. I am very interested to find out the various great warriors or personalities and cultural aspects of our Indian society. So the idea came to my mind to explore the brief history of Baba Farid ji. In this book, I have focused on various achievements of Baba Farid Ji. I am writing this book for our young generation so that when they read this book they will understand the sacrifice and struggle of our forefathers.

CHAPTER ONE

Baba Farid Ji

Baba Farid ji has become a great saint of India. The people of that time were greatly influenced by the lifestyle of Baba Farid ji. There was a lot of sweetness in Farid ji's speech and he used to meet everyone with love and goodwill.

His full name was Fariduddin Shakarganj and he was born in 1173 in Multan, Punjab. He was of saintly nature since childhood, but his mother had a very important contribution in further enhancing his nature. It was his mother who gave direction to Farid ji and made him walk on the path of charity.

When Farid ji began refusing to offer Namaz as a child, his mother made the extremely prudent decision to inculcate the habit in him. His mother assured Farid ji that if he performed the Namaz, Allah would grant him a pleasant reward. Farid ji would sit down to offer Namaz after agreeing to this, and his mother would cleverly maintain a bowl full of sugar nearby as he performed the prayer with his eyes closed. A bowl of sugar would have been in front of Farid ji when he first opened his eyes. Farid ji would have been overjoyed, viewing this as a miracle from Allah, and would have happily ingested sugar.

Farid ji's childhood was blossoming in this manner. After performing namaz, whenever Farid ji opened his eyes, he would occasionally see sweets laying in front of him or sugar in a bowl in front of him. The love Farid ji had for Allah was becoming stronger every day. He now found reading the Namaz to be enjoyable. He has now noticed a spiritual nectar on his tongue.

When Farid ji attained adolescence, he had the need to flee his house and perform penance in the jungle. He was no longer thinking about housework. He merely desired to converge with Allah. He left his house one day and went to the wilderness to perform penance after informing his mother in this manner. He built a little home in the forest and moved there to live. Farid ji made the decision to not pass away till he had attained Allah. He sat in the forest for twelve years as a form of penance as a result of this pledge.

After performing penance for twelve years, Farid ji came home. Farid ji performed a great deal of penance, yet he was unable to accomplish the reason he had gone to the jungle to perform penance. He greeted his mother when he arrived home and told her about his mind's situation. Mother gave Farid ji a hug and urged him to relax. Farid ji was advised to pursue his ambition by his mother. After spending a few days with his mother, Farid Ji prepared to pursue his objective.

Farid Ji was quite enthusiastic after meeting his mother, he again set out for the forest. Farid Ji returned to his cottage. He once again began his devotion in order to see the almighty. During this time of penance, more twelve years passed.

One day as Farid ji was seated in his hut performing morning prayer, a lot of birds began chirping outside. Farid ji's focus was diverted by the constant noises coming from outside, and he became enraged and said, "Die birds." After completing his prayers, Farid ji left the cottage and witnessed a significant number of dead birds. Farid ji was shocked to see everything. Farid Ji cried out, "Birds get up," when he saw the dead birds because he felt bad for them. All the birds rose and took off before Farid Ji could say anything further. Farid ji began to feel accomplished after reading such a sentence. As he saw this wonder of himself, he began to feel proud.

Now that Farid ji has been doing penance for twenty-four years, he has reached the stage where everything he says would come true. Because their predictions always come true, it is stated that sages and saints should never be disregarded.

Farid ji now prepared to go back home. He left the jungle the following day and began to travel back home. While Farid Ji was moving along the road, the ego associated with his abilities began to emerge in his consciousness. While strolling along the street, Farid ji became thirsty. Farid ji noticed a well in the distance. A thirty-year-old girl was watering her crops by getting water from the same well when Farid Ji immediately arrived there. Farid ji asked the girl to fetch some water from the well for him since it was really hot and he was thirsty.

With the utmost respect, the girl advised him to wait because she would first water her crops before giving him water. When Farid ji heard this, he became furious and yelled at the girl, "You don't know me; I have many abilities; I can do whatever I want; and whatever I say becomes true." While continuing to water her fields and listen to Farid Ji's comments, the girl remained silent. Farid ji was enraged at seeing that girl acting so calm and said, "I give you the last warning; Give me water; Otherwise I will kill you."

After hearing what Farid Ji had to say, the girl laughed and remarked, "Will you murder me in the same way that you killed those birds in the jungle?" After hearing this, Farid ji was utterly shocked and began to wonder how he knew that I had killed the sparrows in the forest. The birds were lying dead in front of my home, far from the forest, and I was inside the cottage at the time.

When Farid ji was faced with this dilemma, the girl asked, "What was your purpose when you were sitting on penance twenty-four years ago? What have you accomplished after twenty-four years?" Farid ji's ego was crushed as he listened to that girl, and he also came to realise that she is not a normal young lady.

Farid Ji saw that his aim was still unfulfilled, but he had already given up and was shattered inside. That female then reveals to Farid Ji his biggest fault, which prevented him from arriving at his objective till now.

What was the fault? Farid ji was compassionately informed by that girl that even if you want to work in the world, you must still learn from a Guru, yet you left home to see that God, and that too without a Guru. You have been wandering for twenty-four years because you were not given the correct guidance during initiation from a real Guru.

After hearing this, Farid ji came to the conclusion that not having a Guru was his worst error, and he was now determined to make reparations. He arrived in Multan in quest of a Guru, where he started learning knowledge at a mosque. He was reading a book penned by his father, one day in solitary "Hazrat Khwaja Qutubuddin Bakhtiyar Kaki, came and questioned Farid "What would these medications provide you at this stage"? When Farid saw the face of Bakhtiyar Kaki, he was impressed and turned to him as a master and begged for this benefit. Kaki ji replied, "Farid, you will not get anything from this book."

Farid ji began living his life in accordance with his Guru's instructions as their love for one another grew over time.

There were no flames available in the past to start a fire. People used to put a lot of effort into starting a fire, which would then continue to burn in the kitchen all night. The same fire was used to cook food and heat water next day. Every morning before the sun rose, Farid ji would likewise get up and perform acts of service.

One night it rained a lot, and the stove's fire went out. Farid ji was informed by his master that the fire had been put out due of the previous night's rain when he woke up and went to see him. You travel to the town and bring a house's worth of fire. It continued to rain. The town's streets were completely covered with mud. Unfazed, Farid ji took his blanket and strolled through the puddle-filled pathways to find the fire. Asked at several homes, but the rain had put out the fire in the homes of almost everyone. A home a short distance from the town was now aflame fire. As soon as he arrived, Farid Ji began knocking on the door of the residence.

It was a courtesan's residence. When Farid Ji called, the prostitute quickly became apparent. With a lot of love and respect, Farid ji replied, "Mother, I need fire for cooking at the monastery." Rain caused the fire to go out last night, and because I now desperately need fire, my mentor must be looking over my side. The courtesan then remarked, "My house has a stove in the room itself, therefore there is fire. However, I will offer you this fire only if you give me anything in exchange." The courtesan urged Farid ji to date her since she was so overcome with passion. The courtesan was informed by Farid ji that he did not approve of the agreement. What sort of things are you talking about now that I have granted you the position of mother? I will give you whatever else you ask for, but I won't take this thing you're offering.

Meanwhile, the courtesan thought of a mischief and she told Farid ji that it is okay, you do such a thing that in exchange for this fire, give me one of your eyes and take the fire away. On hearing this, Farid ji picked up a sharp knife lying nearby and gouged out one of his eyes and placed it in front of the courtesan. The courtesan became frightened after watching all of this and began sobbing aloud when she saw Farid ji's eyes in front of her. The courtesan felt terrible about what she had done.

Farid ji's eye was bleeding profusely, and he needed to swiftly return to his master with the fire. He also didn't want his master to find out that I bought the fire by sacrificing my eye. Is. So Farid Ji instantly wrapped his eye with a piece of cloth. After a while, the bleeding stopped, and Farid Ji returned to his monastery.

As soon as he entered the monastery, Farid ji used the same fire to light the stove and begin cooking. Farid ji sat in the same spot and began chanting the name of God after completing all of the tasks. Farid ji's usual routine consisted of his seeing his Guru after he finished cooking, but today he choose not to do so out of concern that Guru ji could learn that one of my eyes is missing. This embodied Farid ji's devotion to his Guru.

When Farid ji failed to show up to see his Guru, his Guru ji questioned his other followers where Farid was because he was nowhere to be found at the time. Guru ji gave his followers the task to find and bring Farid.

A piece of cloth was wrapped over Farid Ji's eye. Guru ji questioned Farid ji about why he had tied the cloth on his eye when he extended out in front of him and showed him the object. Farid ji then retorted that the cloth is knotted since my eye has been in a lot of pain since the morning and isn't opening as a result of the suffering.

After listening to Farid ji, Guru ji said that you remove this cloth from your eyes, your eyes will open. Following the order of his Guru, Farid ji removed that cloth. When Farid ji removed that cloth, a new eye had appeared at that place and the pain had also ended.

Seeing this scene, Farid ji bowed his head at the feet of his Guru and then started worshiping hymns. So these were some priceless stories from the life of Baba Farid ji. I hope you will get to learn a lot from the life of Baba Farid ji. What I have got to learn from Farid ji's life is "patience". Farid ji never lost patience in his entire life. He kept moving forward slowly but surely and finally with the help of his Guru, he got the darshan of the Supreme Father Supreme Soul and got engrossed in chanting the name of the Lord.